My Prayer Closet

A Few Reasons To Pray

A Few Examples Of What To Pray For

A Few Of My Favorite Prayers

A Few People To Pray For

A Quick Lesson On Matthew 6:33

Doing All Things Through Christ

Forcefully Advancing

Firmly Established

Conclusion

©2011 cominus
All rights reserved by the author.
cominus.com

v 1.5

ISBN: 978-1-257-62414-0

The articles in this book originated and were modified between 1994 and 2010 by the author with the same or similar titles.

The author's copyright is only to protect his ability to use his own material. You are free to copy this in part or in full for non commercial uses.

[NASB] - Scripture taken from the NEW AMERICAN STANDARD BIBLE®, Copyright © 1960,1962,1963,1968,1971,1972,1973,1975,1977,1995 by The Lockman Foundation. Used by permission.

[ESV] - Scripture quotations are from The Holy Bible, English Standard Version® (ESV®), copyright © 2001 by Crossway, a publishing ministry of Good News Publishers. Used by permission. All rights reserved.

[NIV 1984] - THE HOLY BIBLE, NEW INTERNATIONAL VERSION®, NIV® Copyright © 1973, 1978, 1984, 2011 by Biblica, Inc.™ Used by permission. All rights reserved worldwide. [We do not endorse the 2011 version.]

Whether thrones or dominions or rulers or authorities--all things were created through [Christ Jesus] and for [Christ Jesus].
[Col 1:16 ESV]

I will perpetuate your memory through all generations; therefore the nations will praise you for ever and ever.
[Psa 45:17 NIV 1984]

INTRODUCTION

This book may appear to be a series of disconnected articles. There is, however, a purpose for presenting these together.

This book begins with three lists about prayers - why we pray, suggested prayer topics, or what to pray for and finishing with my favorite prayers of the Scriptures.

The next article, **A Quick Lesson on Matthew 6:33**, builds upon the topic of prayer. Its purpose is to help us to think deeply about - to discern - what we pray for and what should be our motive in prayer. What does seeking the kingdom of God look like in comparison to our natural desire for personal comfort and building empires, large and small? The purpose of our prayer life is to give glory to God - not to seek glory - or comfort, for ourselves.

Once we have decided we are no longer praying for our own comfort, the next article, **Doing All Things Through Christ**, helps us focus on balancing contentment and setting goals through seeking the kingdom of God.

After we conform our goals to seek the kingdom of God, the next article, *Forcefully Advancing*, helps us understand how to take hold of the kingdom of God and why it is imperative we do so.

The final article, *Firmly Established*, is a call to remember the majesty of our Creator. If we seek the kingdom of God and forcefully take hold of it, our lives will not be invested in our comfort on earth. As we understand the world to be temporal, we will see it for what it is and we will live our lives to exalt our Creator and Savior. Today, we see so many Christians - even Christian leaders - buying in to the dogma of the world and turning the hearts of man to worship the created rather than the Creator.

The Westminster Shorter Catechism no. 1 says, "the chief end of man is to glorify God and enjoy Him forever" and Solomon taught the whole duty of man is to fear God and keep His commandments (Ecc 12:13). Yet the modern American church has invested itself in comfort, syncretizing the faith to make it palatable to the world, instead of seeking to glorify God in all things.

The purpose of this book is to assist you and me in focusing on the authority of Christ and to understand our obligation and opportunity to glorify Him in our prayers and in our walk - in every area of our lives, including our goals and the building of our lives here upon the earth.

"Therefore, as you received Christ Jesus the Lord, so walk in him, rooted and built up in him and established in the faith, just as you were taught, abounding in thanksgiving. See to it that no one takes you captive by philosophy and empty deceit, according to human tradition, according to the elemental spirits of the world, and not according to Christ. For in him the whole fullness of deity dwells bodily, and you have been filled in him, who is the head of all rule and authority." [Col 2:6-10 ESV]

One last thought - or notice - on grammar before we get into the book . . .

In our publications, the use of the pronouns "his," "him," etc. are not always gender specific but may apply equally to the male and/or female party. This use is traditional throughout the history of the English language and female pronouns have been and are always unacceptable for gender-neutral subjects. Therefore, we find it offensive to substitute or join (add) the female gender for gender-neutral subjects ("he or she," "he/she," etc.).

The Bible tells us God made man in His own image (Gen 1:27). We are the image of God and the Bible is specific that He is not a woman. In fact, it was God who coined the term "man" for gender-neutral subjects. "He created them male and female. . . and He called them 'man'." [Gen 5:2; NOTE for KJV: The word for "Adam" in this verse is not a proper noun but is a Hebrew word for "man."] God further demonstrated this principle when, talking to Moses, He referred to "a man or woman" as "he" (Num 5:5-7; 6:1-4).

In this modern politically correct environment, and with modern Christianity wanting to project an inclusive image and a sensitivity to emotional needs (whinings and tantrums), it is easy to go with the flow and change the rendering of our language to fit cultural demands. Most people never consider the history of their language and they are no longer taught the structure of a nations' language has everything to do with their view of God.

Although our nation was founded upon the laws of the Scriptures, we have removed God from almost every arena of life. We find this attempt to substitute female pronouns for gender-neutral subjects, just one more way to remove God from our society. We will not compromise our faith nor our language to satisfy modern political attitudes.

A FEW REASONS TO PRAY

1. Far be it from me that I should sin against the LORD by failing to pray for you. [1Sa 12:23 NIV 1984]

2. If my people who are called by my name humble themselves, and pray and seek my face and turn from their wicked ways, then I will hear from heaven and will forgive their sin and heal their land. [2Ch 7:14 ESV]

3. In the morning, O LORD, You hear my voice; in the morning I lay my requests before You and wait in expectation. [Psa 5:3 NIV 1984]

4. To You they cried out and were delivered; In You they trusted and were not disappointed. [Psa 22:5 NASB]

5. Your face, LORD, do I seek. [Psa 27:8 ESV]

6. This poor man cried, and the LORD heard him and saved him out of all his troubles. [Psa 34:6 ESV]

7. I cry out to God Most High, to God who fulfills his purpose for me. [Psa 57:2 ESV]

8. The horse is made ready for the day of battle, but the victory belongs to the LORD. [Pro 21:31 ESV]

9. I called on your name, O Lord, from the depths of the pit; you heard my plea... You came near when I called on you; you said, 'Do not fear!' You have taken up my cause, O Lord; you have redeemed my life. [Lam 3:55-58 ESV]

10. Watch and pray that you may not enter into temptation. The spirit indeed is willing, but the flesh is weak. [Mar 14:38 ESV]

11. In the same way the Spirit also helps our weakness; for we do not know how to pray as we should, but the Spirit Himself intercedes for us with groanings too deep for words; and He who searches the hearts knows what the mind of the Spirit is, because He intercedes for the

saints according to the will of God. [Rom 8:26-27 NASB]

12. On Him we have set our hope that He will continue to deliver us, as you help us by your prayers. [2Co 1:10-11 NIV 1984]

13. Devote yourselves to prayer, keeping alert in it with an attitude of thanksgiving. [Col 4:2 NASB]

14. Pray without ceasing. [1Th 5:17 NASB]

15. The prayer of a righteous man is powerful and effective. [Jam 5:16 NIV 1984]

16. For the eyes of the Lord are on the righteous and His ears are attentive to their prayer. [1Pe 3:12 NIV 1984]

A FEW EXAMPLES OF WHAT TO PRAY FOR

1. Pray for the peace of Jerusalem. [Psa 122:6 NASB]

2. You who call on the LORD, give yourselves no rest, and give Him no rest till He establishes [Christ's millennial reign in] Jerusalem. [Isa 62:6-7 NIV 1984]

3. Our Father in heaven, hallowed be your name, your kingdom come, your will be done on earth as it is in heaven. [Mat 6:9-10 NASB]

4. Pray earnestly to the Lord of the harvest to send out laborers into his harvest. [Mat 9:38 ESV]

5. Pray that I may be rescued from the unbelievers in Judea and that my service in Jerusalem may be acceptable to the saints there. [Rom 15:31 NIV 1984]

6. I pray that the eyes of your heart may be enlightened, so that you will know

what is the hope of His calling. [Eph 1:18 NASB]

7. I pray that out of His glorious riches He may strengthen you with power through His Spirit in your inner being, so that Christ may dwell in your hearts through faith. [Eph 3:16-17 NIV 1984]

8. Always keep on praying for all the saints. Pray also for me, that whenever I open my mouth, words may be given me so that I will fearlessly make known the mystery of the gospel. [Eph 6:18-19 NIV 1984]

9. And this I pray, that your love may abound still more and more in real knowledge and all discernment. [Php 1:9 NASB]

10. We always thank God, the Father of our Lord Jesus Christ, when we pray for you. [Col 1:3 ESV]

11. And so, from the day we heard, we have not ceased to pray for you, asking that

you may be filled with the knowledge of his will in all spiritual wisdom and understanding, so as to walk in a manner worthy of the Lord, fully pleasing to him, bearing fruit in every good work and increasing in the knowledge of God. [Col 1:9-10 ESV]

12. Night and day we pray most earnestly that we may see you again and supply what is lacking in your faith. [1Th 3:10 NIV 1984]

13. To this end we always pray for you, that our God may make you worthy of his calling and may fulfill every resolve for good and every work of faith by his power, so that the name of our Lord Jesus may be glorified in you, and you in him, according to the grace of our God and the Lord Jesus Christ. [2Th 1:11-12 ESV]

14. Finally, brothers, pray for us that the message of the Lord may spread rapidly and be honored, just as it was with you.

And pray that we may be delivered from wicked and evil men, for not everyone has faith. [2Th 3:1-2 NIV 1984]

15. First of all, then, I urge that supplications, prayers, intercessions, and thanksgivings be made for all people, for kings and all who are in high positions, that we may lead a peaceful and quiet life, godly and dignified in every way. This is good, and it is pleasing in the sight of God our Savior, who desires all people to be saved and to come to the knowledge of the truth. [1Ti 2:1-4 ESV]

16. I pray that you may be active in sharing your faith, so that you will have a full understanding of every good thing we have in Christ. [Phm 1:6 NIV 1984]

A FEW OF MY FAVORITE PRAYERS

1. O LORD, God of Israel, there is no God like you, in heaven above or on earth beneath, keeping covenant and showing steadfast love to your servants who walk before you with all their heart. [1Ki 8:23 ESV]

2. Yours, O LORD, is the greatness and the power and the glory and the majesty and the splendor, for everything in heaven and earth is Yours. Yours, O LORD, is the kingdom; You are exalted as head over all. Wealth and honor come from You; You are the ruler of all things. In Your hands are strength and power to exalt and give strength to all. Now, our God, we give You thanks and praise Your glorious name. [1Ch 29:11-13 NIV 1984]

3. LORD, there is no one like You to help the powerless against the mighty. Help us, O LORD our God, for we rely on You. [2Ch 14:11 NIV 1984]

4. O Lord God of heaven, the great and awesome God who keeps covenant and steadfast love with those who love him and keep his commandments, let your ear be attentive and your eyes open, to hear the prayer of your servant. [Neh 1:5-6 ESV]

5. Blessed be Your glorious name, and may it be exalted above all blessing and praise. You alone are the LORD. You made the heavens, even the highest heavens, and all their starry host, the earth and all that is on it, the seas and all that is in them. You give life to everything, and the multitudes of heaven worship You. [Neh 9:5-6 NIV 1984]

6. When I am afraid, I will put my trust in You. In God, whose word I praise, In God I have put my trust; I shall not be afraid. What can mere man do to me? [Psa 56:3-4 NASB]

7. Say to God, "How awesome are your deeds! So great is your power that your enemies come cringing to you. All the earth worships you and sings praises to you; they sing praises to your name." [Psa 66:3-4 ESV]

8. The heavens are Yours, and Yours also the earth; You founded the world and all that is in it. You created the north and the south; Your arm is endued with power; Your hand is strong, Your right hand exalted. Righteousness and justice are the foundation of Your throne; love and faithfulness go before You. Blessed are those who have learned to acclaim You, who walk in the light of Your presence, O LORD. They rejoice in Your name all day long; they exult in Your righteousness. For You are their glory and strength, and by Your favor You exalt our horn. [Psa 89:11-17 NIV 1984]

9. I will give thanks to you, O Lord, among the peoples; I will sing praises to you among the nations. For your steadfast

love is great above the heavens; your faithfulness reaches to the clouds. Be exalted, O God, above the heavens! Let your glory be over all the earth! [Psa 108:3-5 ESV]

10. O LORD, You are my God; I will exalt You, I will give thanks to Your name; For You have worked wonders, Plans formed long ago, with perfect faithfulness. [Isa 25:1 NASB]

11. O LORD, be gracious to us; we wait for you. Be our arm every morning, our salvation in the time of trouble. [Isa 33:2 ESV]

12. Do any of the worthless idols of the nations bring rain? Do the skies themselves send down showers? No, it is You, O LORD our God. Therefore our hope is in You, for You are the One who does all this. [Jer 14:22 NIV 1984]

13. Ah, Lord GOD! It is you who has made the heavens and the earth by your great power and by your outstretched arm!

Nothing is too hard for you. [Jer 32:17 ESV]

14. You, O Lord, reign forever; your throne endures from generation to generation. . . Restore us to yourself, O Lord, that we may return; renew our days as of old - unless you have utterly rejected us, and are angry with us beyond measure. [Lam 5:19-22 NIV 1984]

15. Blessed be the name of God forever and ever, to whom belong wisdom and might. He changes times and seasons; he removes kings and sets up kings; he gives wisdom to the wise and knowledge to those who have understanding; he reveals deep and hidden things; he knows what is in the darkness, and the light dwells with him. To you, O God of my fathers, I give thanks and praise. [Dan 2:20-23 ESV]

16. For we do not present our pleas before you because of our righteousness, but

because of your great mercy. [Dan 9:18 ESV]

17. LORD, I have heard of Your fame; I stand in awe of Your deeds, O LORD. Renew them in our day, in our time make them known; in wrath remember mercy. [Hab 3:2 NIV 1984]

18. Worthy are You, our Lord and our God, to receive glory and honor and power; for You created all things, and because of Your will they existed, and were created. [Rev 4:11 NASB]

19. Great and amazing are your deeds, O Lord God the Almighty! Just and true are your ways, O King of the nations! Who will not fear, O Lord, and glorify your name? For you alone are holy. All nations will come and worship you, for your righteous acts have been revealed. [Rev 15:3-4 ESV]

A FEW PEOPLE TO PRAY FOR

Family & Relatives

Friends & Neighbors

Unsaved Friends

Church Pastors & Leaders

Elected Officials & Bureaucrats

Business and Work Associates

Our Persecuted Brothers

A QUICK LESSON ON MATTHEW 6:33

"Therefore do not be anxious, saying, 'What shall we eat?' or 'What shall we drink?' or 'What shall we wear?'... But seek first the kingdom of God and his righteousness, and all these things will be added to you. Therefore do not be anxious about tomorrow, for tomorrow will be anxious for itself. Sufficient for the day is its own trouble." [Mat 6:31-34 ESV]

The beginning portion of the Lord's Prayer (Mat 6:9-13) includes the phrase, "Your kingdom come, Your will be done." This is speaking of God's kingdom. But it is natural in our flawed, human existence to be preoccupied with our own kingdom. Instead of praying for God's will, we often pray "my will be done" - even if those are not the exact words.

When our prayers are focused around our own needs and goals, we are not seeking the kingdom - or God's will. When we are confident for provision from our own industry and talent, we are not seeking the kingdom of God. When we worry for lack of comfort - when we trust in what we can see and touch - we are not seeking the kingdom of God.

The Pharisees wanted a location for this kingdom - something they could see and touch (Luke 17:20-37). Jesus' response was the kingdom was in their midst - that is, it is within those who believe.

Then Jesus turned to His disciples and instructed them on the coming of the Son (His future second coming). He warned them to pay no attention to people who claim He has come and is here or there, because when He comes, we will need no one to tell us. Christ will come riding in the clouds and the heavens will announce His presence (see also the companion passage in Mat 24).

Christ told the disciples, when He comes it will be just like it was when Noah walked into the ark and when Lot fled Sodom: everyone will be doing what they always did before. Eating, and drinking and chasing after a comfortable life.

Then Christ explained the test that would prove those who are seeking after the kingdom: He said, if you are on the roof and you see the Son of Man coming, don't go into your house to retrieve your stuff. The same goes if you are in the field - forget your stuff. Remember Lot's wife. When commanded to flee the city, she paused to look back on her comfortable life and she was turned to a pillar of salt. If you live to keep your comfortable life - or your stuff - you will lose eternal life (Luk 17:30-35).

What is important? Do we seek after the latest fashion? Do we long for a new car? or house? If we are seeking the kingdom of God, we will not be worried about these things - or our collection of stuff. When we hear the heavens rolling and witness the catastrophe announcing Christ's return, will we run back into the house to grab our computer? or jewels? or gold and silver coins?

Regardless all this instruction - after Jesus rebuked the Pharisees for looking for a location and time and explaining His return with great warning to the disciples - nonetheless, the disciples also wanted a location. They did not grasp the urgency of seeking the kingdom, they sought what they could see and touch. So Christ replied, "Where the corpse is, there the vultures will gather." [Luk 17:37 ESV] That our minds are even on our stuff after Christ's graphic description of His return is a demonstration of the death that easily grips our lives. Using this illustration, Jesus affirms, we don't need to know the location - if we look to the sky, it will be obvious when He returns. Or, you could take it another way - when you see the vultures - the sign of the end, know that your stuff - your comfort - is dead.

Where there is death, destruction will follow - and it will be obvious for all to see. We live in a fallen, dying world and we know there is no purpose in struggling for a comfortable life, or to build our kingdom down here. But we strive for it anyway - we succumb to the natural tendency to worry about our comfort here on earth. When we do this, we are not seeking the Kingdom of God. In fact, Christ says we are following the ways of the pagans (Mat 6:32). To seek first the Kingdom of God is to lay aside our stuff - our goals and our small empires - and "worry" about God's stuff.

What is God's stuff? Do I crave the presence of God (Psa 16:11; 51:10-12)? Do I marvel in His awesome works (Psa 66:3-7)? Have I been a witness with my life and my words today (Mat 28:18-20)? Have I helped those God put in my path (Gal 6:2)? Am I looking forward to Christ's return (Psa 122:6, Isa 62:6-7) - do I want Him to return right now? Am I praying for God's Kingdom, or my kingdom (Mat 6:9-10)? Am I standing boldly for the truth of the Gospel of Jesus Christ and the doctrines of the Scriptures (Eph 6:10-19; 1Ti 4:16)?

The Apostle Peter warned us that everything in this world, including all our hopes and dreams and stuff, will be destroyed. Then he asked, "What kind of people ought you to be?" [2Pe 3:11] We ought to live holy, godly lives - seeking first the Kingdom of God. Peter explained that is how we speed Christ's coming.

If we love God, we look forward to a new heaven and a new earth - the home of righteousness, not stuff - where we will enjoy God forever.

DOING ALL THINGS THROUGH CHRIST

One of the great motivational verses of the Scriptures is, "I can do all things through Christ who gives me strength." [Php 4:13] Some Christians claim this as their "life verse."

Most often, this verse is used within the context of striving for higher achievement and the hope of attaining it with God's help. I have been to motivational meetings, filled with Christians, where this verse is affirmed over and over. Another common use is when Christians talk of trials and adversity, or beginning new and difficult ventures. This verse is the common response given by others as encouragement, hoping to be helpful and plant seeds of positive attitudes.

Recently, my wife and I were attending a business network meeting. It was supposed to be a meeting of business people but it turned out to be a class on setting goals. The facilitator asked us to draw a pyramid and at the top of the pyramid we were to segregate a section and call that our vision. Our vision is where we want to be in the next three years; lifestyle, vacations, money and the works. How do we arrive at this vision? According to the facilitator, we arrive there from our discontent: we refuse to accept the state in which we find ourselves and decide to set new goals for a better life.

Have you ever been to a Multi-Level Marketing (MLM) meeting? or a Positive Motivation (PMA) meeting? The strategy upline use to recruit downline sales teams is to instill a desire to excel financially. How do they do this? By creating discontent with the financial state people find themselves and the promise that hard work - and only four hours per week - will catapult them into a life of wealth, ease and residual income.

Discontent is a great motivator. Even the well meaning Christian is unwittingly giving permission for being discontent when using this verse to encourage another to rise above their present state or circumstances.

This does not mean it is necessarily wrong to be discontent, or to set goals. The reason for our discontent and the result of our goals determine whether we are seeking to follow Christ or trying to conform His plans to ours.

What did Paul mean, when he said he could do all things through Christ? To find out, we must read the context of the verse. Just two verses up we find he is talking about being content in every situation - whether poor and hungry or rich and well fed. And it is because of this contentment in Christ he is able to do everything, or suffer through every situation he finds himself. He is content to be where God wants him to be and is not frustrated about unreached goals.

"[F]or I have learned to be content whatever the circumstances. I know what it is to be in need, and I know what it is to have plenty. I have learned the secret of being content in any and every situation, whether well fed or hungry, whether living in plenty or in want. I can do everything through him who gives me strength." [Php 4:11-13 NIV 1984]

Twice - two times - Paul tells us he has learned contentment - and it did not come naturally just because he was an apostle. It is easy to be content in wealth and ease, so circumstances would imply Paul had to go through testing, times of want and hunger, to learn contentment. How do you handle testing? I fail most times of testing - I become discontent and want to raise myself above the circumstances. But it is this testing Paul is talking about - not the high goals of accomplishment or of a better life - when he says he can do all things and that Christ gives him strength.

This does not necessarily mean we are to abandon all our goals, or we do not strive to excel. First, we know from Christ's prayer (John 17), we live in the world but are not of this world. This means our goals should not establish our lives down here but should work to advance our life in the kingdom - or God's will. Second, the Scriptures tell us whatever we do, to do as unto the Lord (Col 3:17). This means the purpose of our life is to please God and accomplish what He has predetermined he wants us to do (Eph 2:10). So, in the second place, we excel in whatever God has given us to do - doing everything for Him. This brings us to the first place - keeping our eyes on the kingdom of God.

If our goal is to increase in wealth, we are staking our claim down here and not seeking the kingdom. This does not mean it is wrong to establish businesses, nor is it wrong to gain wealth. Our motivation, intent and attitude make for right or wrong. Are we looking for our glory and comfort, or God's glory and His will? Do we seek to be where God wants us to be?

Proverbs tells us man makes his plans but God directs his steps. [Pro 16:9] Before we were born, God appointed our steps - He had a plan for our lives (Isa 49:1; Jer 1:5) and He numbered our days (Psa 139:16). Most of us have plans for our lives. Do we seek to conform our plans to God's will, or do we seek to conform God's plans to our will?

For Paul to learn contentment, he had to face many trials. James, the brother of Jesus, wrote we should count it all joy when we face trials because the testing of our faith develops patience, perseverance or endurance - or contentment (Jam 1:2). The writer of the Book of Hebrews tells us in chapter twelve, God sends discipline to the sons He loves. Our discipline, or testing, is to teach us and train us to live the life God wants us to live - to be where God wants us to be - and to be content in that position.

Before Paul was saved, Christ spoke to him and said he was kicking against the goads (Act 26:14). A goad keeps an animal in check, to get them to do what the owner wants - to accomplish the owner's goals.

Kicking against the goads is futile because the owner is going to direct the animal. Paul's life, to that point, was futile and most our lives are spent in similar futility. God holds the goads and He was steering Paul, just as He steers us. But like all people - like you and me - Paul resisted God's plan and His ways (Rom 3:11-12).

Although Paul thought he was living his life for God, nothing could have been further from the truth (Php 3:4-9). How often do we rush headlong into life thinking, seeking, or even determined, we are doing God's will, only to discover we have made a mess of ourselves and our witness?

After Paul received Christ, he left everything behind - every accomplishment and every goal he counted as loss (Php 3:7). Paul's strength was in Christ - knowing in poverty or wealth, Christ was going to help him walk in God's plan.

Paul had a plan to travel to Spain (Rom 15:24) but he never made it. Yet, he never recorded a lament for missed goals. Instead, he wrote we are to make it our goal to please God (2Co 5:9) and we press on to win the prize - seeking the kingdom, that is (Php 3:14). This is where he found contentment. His life did not consist of what he built for himself down here. Instead, his purpose was to be where God wanted him to be - pursuing the kingdom of God.

You and I are saved by grace (Eph 2:8-9) and justified by faith (Rom 5:1) - we can add nothing to it (Tit 3:5). This is who we are in Christ - this is what it means to be a Christian. We rest in what Christ has done for us - not in what we can do for Him. Contentment comes from knowing who we are in Christ and leaving our goals behind.

We know God has a plan for our life; we know God directs our steps; we know He disciplines us to lead us in the right direction; and we know He is everything we need, He is our strength - we do not need the strength or comfort of this world.

Therefore, we set goals for the kingdom and fit our lives around those goals, knowing whatever state we find ourselves in, whether rich and well fed, whether poor and hungry, whether in favor or in adversity, we can do all things through Christ who gives us strength. Our goal is not our comfort. Our goal is to be where God wants us to be and to glorify Him in whatever we do - in whatever state we find ourselves.

FORCEFULLY ADVANCING

When God asks who will represent Him to a people who will not listen, will we, like Isaiah, volunteer to go (Isa 6:8)?

Some Christians claim their faith is a personal matter. Christ said we do not light a lamp to hide it (Mat 5:15) and David wrote, "I have not hidden Your righteousness within my heart; I have spoken of Your faithfulness and Your salvation." [Psa 40:10 NASB] What David and Christ are saying, is our faith in Christ is not a personal matter - we will broadcast it and it will affect the lives of all those around us.

Christ gave us further instructions to declare to the world the authority of Christ, making disciples, baptizing them in public display and teaching them to obey Christ's commands (Mat 28:18-20). Based upon Scripture, we can only conclude a sincere faith in Christ is not a private matter.

Some Christians are willing to stand up for what they view as the Gospel but are unwilling to stand up when the truth of God's Word is under attack. They rationalize this position by limiting their witness to salvation issues and/or by assigning cultural issues to politics and out of the realm of the Gospel. They believe the role of the Christian is to be kind and non-judgmental. Like the world, they view any stand for truth as arrogant and hateful. All-the-while, the majority of Christians are working hard to build a comfortable life down here and do not recognize the war that life is.

Satan has rallied kings to advance the world toward death (Psa 2). We see the fruit of this conspiracy throughout our culture - and Christians lament as they see the kingdom of death advancing. Yet, Christ has promised He will triumph (1Co 15:24). While on earth, He said, "The kingdom of heaven has been forcefully advancing and forceful men lay hold of it." [Mat 11:12] There is a war between advancing kingdoms - and one side has already won.

You and I are in this war. Will we fight on the frontlines, or advance to the rear? Martin Luther said, "If I profess with the loudest voice and clearest exposition every portion of the truth of God except precisely that little point which the world and the devil are at that moment attacking, I am not confessing Christ, however boldly I may be professing Christ. Where the battle rages, there the loyalty of the soldier is proved, and to be steady on all battlefields besides, is mere flight and disgrace if he flinches at that point."

Where is this battle line drawn today? Church and culture are caught in confusion: they have embraced evolution as fact and killing unborn babies as a woman's right to choose. One of the problems with the theory of evolution is the doctrine of natural selection. The same people who profess this doctrine, that nature decides which species survives, also claim it is mans' responsibility to protect "endangered" species. This dichotomy is further complicated by mans' refusal to protect his own species in the womb. We are confused only because we have rejected the truth of the Word of God.

Evil has a purpose in the confusion: If we can explain creation by evolution, we have no need for a Creator. If there is no Creator, then there is no higher law than man. Or, if that Creator has allowed nature to evolve, then He has distanced Himself from creation and has allowed man to become his own authority for law. Or, by relegating the creation story and the fall of man to myth we can scientifically deny original sin and we have no need for a Savior.

Going green is another battlefield confusing the culture and church. If we maintain mans' obligation to protect the so-called endangered species and even that the whole planet is within mans' power and obligation to protect, we can thereby deny that God sustains the earth. Despite the fact that the Bible tells us Christ sustains all creation by His Word (Heb 1:3) and God has promised the earth cannot be moved (Gen 8:22; Psa 93:1; 96:10).

When we stand with the world, we nullify God's law and authority by negating His claim as Creator and Sustainer. Additionally we justify slothful behavior, which is the opposite of His command to subdue the resources and be productive (Gen 1:28; 9:1). Confusing preserving the earth and sustainability with stewardship constrains man from fulfilling his thankful obligation to God to subdue the resources He has given us and robs God of His glory.

Don't be surprised that America - which was established upon the doctrines of the Christian faith and whose Founding Fathers believed it was the destiny of this nation to bring the Gospel of Jesus Christ to the world - has now succumbed to a pantheistic worldview that includes all faiths while seeking to exclude faith in Jesus Christ. The church has refused to confront paganism in the culture. Our churches have syncretized the doctrines to please the dogmas of the world.

Aaron did this with the golden calf in the thirty-second chapter of Exodus. The people were tired of waiting for Moses. They wanted gods and leadership to advance them forward - not make them wait around in a hot desert. Aaron, the priest appointed by God Himself, was afraid of the people. So he fashioned the calf, declared it to be their god and proclaimed a festival to the LORD. He syncretized: he gave the people the god they wanted while proclaiming a festival, or worship, to the true God.

This is the way of the modern church as it tries to please both God and man. "So while these nations feared the LORD, they also served their idols " [2Ki 17:41 NASB] The lie calls sin and rebellion "diversity" and promotes a tolerance of evil. We need to understand that truth brings division. Jesus Christ said, "Do not think that I came to bring peace on earth. I did not come to bring peace but a sword." [Mat 10:34 NKJV]

Jesus warned that if the light within us is darkness – or man's light, which only leads to more sin no matter what goodness is espoused – then how great is that darkness (Mat 6:23). To syncretize falsehood to truth can only produce serious error. Christ said if we follow after Him, then we will know the truth and be set free of our confusion (Joh 8:31-32). We must return to the Scriptures as the written authority for all of life.

The foundation of freedom is truth. As Christians, we become entangled with - or enslaved to - the world through compromise and tolerance (Heb 12:1; 2Pe 2:20) or we can be that city set on a hill (Mat 5:14-16). There is no freedom without truth. There is no truth without Christ.

So, getting back to what Jesus Christ said about the war we find ourselves in, "From the days of John the Baptist until now, the kingdom of heaven has been forcefully advancing, and forceful men lay hold of it." [Mat 11:12 NIV 1984] Or, "the kingdom of heaven suffers violence and the violent take it by force." [adapted from other versions]

Before we break this down, let me explain why I do not hold to the interpretation that "suffers violence" and "violent take it by force" refer to violence done to the kingdom.

First) Christ dated this "from the days of John the Baptist." At the time of his teaching, John the Baptist was still alive. Clearly, Christ was not speaking of the violence done to John via the beheading. Also, the kingdom of heaven has been exposed to attacks since the early days of man when Cain killed Abel (Gen 4:8; Mat 23:33-39; Luk 11:47-52). So, there was a larger reason Jesus dated this from the days of John the Baptist.

Second) Because Christ dated this "from the days of John the Baptist" and John was still alive, He must have meant since he began preaching "the kingdom of heaven is near (Mat 3:2)." This implies the kingdom of heaven has been advancing from this time - the time of the Messiah.

Third) The context: In the previous chapter, Christ sent out the disciples to proclaim, "The kingdom of heaven is near." In His instructions, he warned that in the future, they would be brought before magistrates and councils and men would hate them because of Christ, whom they represented. Yet, He also instructed them to heal the sick and other such manifestations of the kingdom and that those who oppose them would face the severest judgment. And when they are brought before man, the Holy Spirit will give them the words to speak. He instructed them that whoever stood firm to the end would be saved and not to be afraid. So, the previous chapter cannot be solely lent to the side of confirming the kingdom of heaven suffers attack. If anything, the previous chapter is a confirmation that we are in a spiritual war. And Christ summed this up when He said He did not come to bring peace, but a sword (Mat 10:34).

Fourth) More context: as mentioned above, in the previous chapter, Christ sent the disciples out to preach "The kingdom of heaven is near." Chapter eleven begins by explaining Christ had just sent out the disciples when He moved on to other towns to preach and was met by John's disciples to present questions to Christ to relieve John's doubts. To this, Christ answered with a description of the manifestations of the kingdom. As John's disciples leave, Jesus asked the people about John and He affirms John to be a prophet, specifically, that John was preparing the way before Christ - the messenger of the Messiah and then He commends John's life and says, "From the days of John the Baptist, the kingdom of heaven has been forcefully advancing." Then He speaks to the people's confusion that the kingdom has, in fact, come but they cannot see it and ends with a pronouncement of woes upon the cities that rejected the manifestations of the kingdom and an offer of rest for those who believe.

Fifth) The word "suffers" in the KJV and other translations, according to Strong's Concordance, does not mean something inflicted upon or endured by the kingdom. According to Strong's the words "suffers violence" (biazo) means to force. A respondent may crowd into, or passively, to seize - to take hold of, or grasp. The root of this word is bios, which is translated life, or the present state of existence, by implication, the means of that life. Thus, the state of the kingdom of heaven is force - or advancing.

This violence Christ spoke of, as in "the violent take it by force" or "forceful men lay hold of it," I believe He alluded to it when describing the character of John the Baptist in verse seven (Mat 11:7). John was not a reed swayed by the wind. He was resolute and never compromised God's law - he did not blow with the winds of culture; he did not syncretize the faith to make it more attractive to the world - he stood up and was not afraid to be counted on the side of God. He did not fear man - who could only kill him - but feared the One who could "destroy both soul and body in hell." [Mat 10:34 NASB] John is our example of violence, or forcefulness. He took hold of the kingdom, even to the death.

John the Baptist was not afraid to call the people to repent - he did not preach a gospel of love - and he was not afraid to hold public officials accountable for their private sins. The truth - the gospel - he upheld was violent against the world's system. In this same way, Christ has called us to become violent - this is not a physical violence against man. Truth is a violence against the world and all the principalities who are in rebellion to God. We are violent by boldly proclaiming God's truth.

"For the word of God is living and active, sharper than any two-edged sword, piercing to the division of soul and of spirit, of joints and of marrow, and discerning the thoughts and intentions of the heart. And no creature is hidden from his sight, but all are naked and exposed to the eyes of him to whom we must give account." [Heb 4:12-13 ESV]

The Word of God is a sword (Eph 6:17). We do not wage spiritual warfare with the weapons of the world (2Co 10:3-4). The Bible tells us in 2Co 10:5 our weapons have divine power to demolish every argument and every claim that sets itself up against the knowledge of God. We are commanded to, take captive every thought and make it obedient to Christ. Paul warned us not to be taken captive by the principles of this world (Col 2:8); to resist conforming to the world and be transformed by the renewing of our minds (Rom 12:2). We are in a war and our weapon is the Bible. If we wish to become skilled and ready for battle, we must spend time studying the Word.

If someone told you becoming a Christian would result in a comfortable life, I am here to inform you that you were deceived. My friend, when we receive Christ, we are called to obey (Luk 11:28; Joh 14:23; Eph 2:8-10). This obedience to God is violence to the world - it opposes the world and the world opposes it. This means, we are in a war.

In Matthew chapter eleven, when Jesus said "forceful men lay hold of it," implicit in this illustration is a call to hold forth the truth - because His kingdom is advancing.

If Peter admonished us to live Godly lives to speed the day of the Lord (2Pe 3:11) and Christ declared the end will not come until the whole world has heard the gospel (Mat 24:14), then how can a Christian even think of aiding the world's agenda by promoting the world's systems - a culture and law based upon feelings - or, for that matter, establishing a comfortable life?

Paul told us in Ephesians chapter six that after we have done everything to stand, stand and stand firm. You and I must be faithful (1Co 15:1-2). Nowhere in Scripture are we commanded to win - but the Bible tells us Jesus has already won (Luk 10:18).

Christ was sent to this world to crush Satan's head and remove his dominion (Gen 3:15; Luk 10:18; Joh 12:31; Rom 16:20). The Apostle John claimed that Christ came to destroy Satan's work (1Jo 3:8). Christ declared, "The prince of this world now stands condemned." [Joh 16:11 NIV 1984] Satan has lost. We may feel overwhelmed as we see evil schemes and conspiracies advancing but Satan cannot prevail against the cause of Christ. Jesus told us the kingdom of heaven is forcefully advancing.

As we take our positions in this war, our duty is to stand against the schemes of the devil - being strong in the Lord. We do not struggle against flesh and blood but against spiritual forces in the heavenly realms (Eph 6:10-17). When we stand for truth of God's Word, we do violence to the world's system and among the principalities and we glorify God on earth.

FIRMLY ESTABLISHED

In the Bible, in the Book of Revelation, chapter four, the Apostle John describes a scene in heaven. It is a picture of Christ sitting on the throne, ruling over all things. There is no question - He is God. Christ reigns in glory and majesty and John tries to describe the scene, the colors, the brilliance, the sounds and the splendor, which words cannot begin to express.

Around the throne are twenty-four smaller thrones: smaller rulers - but important enough to be seated in the presence of God. There are four creatures awesome in description - they are great, powerful and fearsome. The picture is of an awesome, indescribable, powerful God surrounded by twenty-four kings and four fearsome creatures full of eyes and wings, crying out in praise to God. Meanwhile, the creatures never stop saying, "Holy, holy, holy is the Lord God Almighty, who was, and is, and is to come." [Rev 4:8] And John wrote whenever the living creatures give Christ glory, the twenty-four kings fall on their faces before Him, submitting their authority to Him and they worship Him.

The Bible tells us God raises kings and topples them (Dan 2:21) and Jesus said all power, or authority to rule, is given by God above (Joh 19:11). The kings in heaven understand this and they submit to Christ in worship crying out, "You are worthy, our Lord and God, to receive glory and honor and power, for you created all things, and by your will they were created and have their being." [Rev 4:11 NIV 1984]

One day, we will witness the majesty of God and we will be repeating these words. We will praise God - God the Father, God the Son and God the Holy Spirit - because He alone is worthy of praise, He alone is God - He is the creator of all things and all things were created because He planned it (Isa 25:1). It is only through Him that all things exist and all life is sustained (Heb 1:3). And the Bible tells us, every knee will bow and every tongue will confess Jesus Christ is Lord. All mankind will declare Him King of kings, to the glory of God the Father (Php 2:10-11).

This Christ is the majesty who created all things (Joh 1:3). Psalm 33:6 tells us God made the heavens by His word and all the stars and planets were made by His breath. Hebrews 1:3 tells us that Christ keeps everything in its place by His word. And He has told us the earth is firmly established, it cannot be moved - it cannot be destroyed by man (Gen 8:22; Psa 93:1; 78:69; 95:4,5; 96:10; 104:5; 119:90; Ecc 1:4).

God is in control. There is no man - nor is there a conspiracy of men - who can defeat His will, or His plan. It takes a great imagination to think the created could overturn, or defeat, the Creator. Logic and reason will tell you it is impossible.

But the conversation within church and culture is about how man is destroying the planet. Global warming, saving the planet and going green are mantras continually drummed into our conversation. We have deceived ourselves to believe we are powerful enough to destroy what God says we cannot. Under the mask of environmental stewardship, more and more professing Christians are being won over to the argument that we must work to preserve the earth - to save it from human destruction. The Gospel is being syncretized to make it palatable to the world and few Christians take the time to understand what the Bible has to say about the matter.

What does the Bible say about mans' responsibility to the earth? Let's start with what God instructed the first man, Adam. He told him to, "Be fruitful and multiply and fill the earth and subdue it and have dominion over the fish of the sea and over the birds of the heavens and over every living thing that moves on the earth." [Gen 1:28 ESV] Breaking this down, we find God told man to have a lot of babies, live all over the land and learn to use all the resources of the earth, mastering the fish, birds and animals.

If we look at this Scripture closer, we see God gave man dominion over the earth and the authority to rule over every living creature.

1. God did not make man equal to or less than the earth He said "fill it up with people and use up the resources." Contrary to conventional wisdom, man is not blight upon the earth. "The earth He has given to man." [Psa 115:16 NIV 1984]

2. God did not make man equal to or less than the animals. He gave man wisdom and knowledge to rule over the animals. We have permission - the authority - to use animals for food, as equipment, for research and we can even tell them where to live. We do not owe the animals our choice habitat.

God told Adam He did not create the earth to be empty, pristine or preserved, but to be inhabited all over the face of it. That means "urban sprawl" is God's choice (see also Isa 45:18).

After God destroyed the earth with a flood (Gen 6-7), He made a special promise to Noah, "While the earth remains, seedtime and harvest, cold and heat, summer and winter, day and night, shall not cease." [Gen 8:22 ESV] God gave no caution or instruction for responsible or sustainable use. The seasons will come in their course and global warming will not stop that.

If the earth is firmly established, as God says it is, then it follows the earth is not fragile. In fact, it has proven to be very hardy. Even environmental disasters that we throw billions of dollars into cleaning up, we find the bulk of the cleaning is performed by the earth - or by God's hand in nature. Forty years ago, when I was in high school, Lake Erie was known as the most polluted body of water in the world. We were told in our textbooks it would take two hundred to four hundred years to clean it up. But when the pollution activity stopped, it took only a few short years and the work of the earth far out-paced the billions of dollars we sunk into the project. Today, Lake Erie is one of the cleanest lakes in the world. Man cannot destroy what God has created.

Was preserving the earth on the mind of Christ? Peter was a disciple of Christ. He was with the Lord all day long, evenings and weekends, eating, talking, laughing and listening to everything Christ heard from His Father and revealed to them. With all that, neither Peter nor any other disciple ever mentioned the need to help the earth. It is safe to assume, stewardship of the earth's resources was not on the mind of Christ at all - not for that time; not for the future. Quite the opposite, in fact, Peter reminds us that God destroyed the world by water, and in the future, He intends to destroy it by fire (2Pe 3:5-7 see also Job 22:15-20).

Man was created in the image of God (Gen 1:27). We reflect this image in many ways. One way we reflect God's image is in production. By living in obedience to God and producing useful products from the resources of the earth given by God's goodness, we reflect God's image as Creator. He creates out of nothing and we create using the resources He has given us. We are sub-creators, if you will.

But Satan has set out to deceive man from the start - and his work is aided by man's rebellious heart. We live in a culture of victim hood where no man is responsible to law for his own actions. Our laws and our lawmakers look at ways to punish the producers and limit our reproduction - even financing the killing of our children in the womb. We are deceived - and even professing Christians are aiding the enemy in this war.

"For they exchanged the truth of God for a lie, and worshiped and served the creature rather than the Creator, who is blessed forever. Amen." [Rom 1:25 NASB]

One of the most important things to God is mans' relationship to his Creator and Savior - that man will glorify God and enjoy Him forever. One of the most important things we can do is to proclaim His glory among men. When we support efforts to "go green" we delude this message of truth and adopt the pagan priority of saving the planet, which God tells us He - and He alone - is going to destroy. God has no love for the earth - in the end He will have destroyed it twice.

Man's first commission was to produce - and this has never been revoked. Christ's commission to His followers is to broadcast His authority and the message of salvation. When we focus on saving the earth, we violate both commissions and surrender ground to Satan and his pagan demons.

God tells us the earth is firmly established. Let us be firmly established in Him by diligently searching His Word and giving Him praise among men (Col 1:23).

CONCLUSION

May these articles spur you on to dedicating your life and your goals to glorifying God. May you seek God in prayer daily - constantly - praying for His will to be done on earth and in your life. May you lay down the pursuit of your empire and comfort for the pursuit of His will. May you find contentment in being where God wants you to be. May you learn to take hold of the kingdom. And, finally, may you stand up against the deception in the world - the deception which seeks to rob God of His glory. May you seek God's strength in holding forth the Word of Truth.

If you do not know God, know this, all truth is in His Son, Jesus Christ (Joh 8:31-32), who came to earth to die - to save us from our sins and He rose from the dead to give us eternal life (Joh 3:16). You must repent of your sins and believe on the Lord Jesus Christ to be saved (Act 3:19-20; 16:30; Rom 10:9-10). If you believe Christ, you will follow Him (Mat 16:34; Joh 10:4; 12:26). It is as simple as that.

God is prolife.